WOMEN IN BLUE-COLLAR JOBS

A Ford Foundation Conference Report

Library of Congress Cataloging in Publication Data
Main entry under title:

Women in blue-collar jobs.

Summary of the Conference on Women in Blue-Collar Industrial and Service Jobs held at the Ford Foundation in December, 1974.
1. Women—Employment—United States— Congresses. 2. Labor and laboring classes— United States—Congresses. I. Conference on Women in Blue-Collar Industrial and Service Jobs, Ford Foundation, 1974. II. Ford Foundation.
HD6095.W69   331.4'0973   76-2499

ISBN 0-916584-01-1

CONTENTS

INTRODUCTION

Most women work because they have to. Almost half of all working women in the United States are single, widowed, divorced, or living with husbands who have incomes of less than $7,000 a year. Yet the limited research that has been done on the working woman has concentrated on the higher-status "professionals," a group that constitutes only a very small part of the female work force.

Working-class women have largely been ignored, even though their proportion in the American work force has increased from about 18 per cent of all workers in 1900 to 40 per cent in 1974. There are a great many studies of blue-collar workers, but almost all of them assume blue-collar workers to be men. Thus the research deals with working conditions, the degree of job satisfaction, and occupational security, but not such matters as day-care facilities for workers' children.

For the past few years the Ford Foundation has been interested in both the problems of blue-collar workers generally, and in the changing role of women in American society.* In the belief that the needs of working-class women and their families must be carefully analyzed before they can be met adequately, the Foundation convened a two-day national Conference on Women in Blue-Collar Industrial and Service Jobs in December, 1974.

The conference was suggested and organized by Joyce L. Kornbluh of the University of Michigan's Institute of Labor and Industrial Relations, Pamela Roby of the University of California (Santa Cruz), and Barbara Wertheimer of Cornell University's School of Industrial and Labor Relations. They were assisted at the Foundation by Kathryn Mitchell of the National Affairs Division. Forty-three people from a variety of social science, educational, labor, and community institutions participated. (See Appendix, p. 26.)

Some of the problems discussed at the conference are the same today as those that have beset working women for two or three generations. Others

---

*The Foundation has supported a range of research and action projects related to the quality of working life. It has also supported studies of sex discrimination in employment and education, assisted groups concerned with the legal rights and special needs of poor minority women, and helped launch the Trade Union Women's Studies Program, conducted by the Cornell School of Industrial and Labor Relations. (See *That 51 Per Cent: Ford Foundation Activities Related to Opportunities for Women*, available from the Ford Foundation, Office of Reports, 320 East 43 Street, New York, N.Y. 10017.)

are new: People are generally more affluent, which has made possible wider educational opportunities for women as well as men; labor-saving devices have increased leisure time and also freed more women to work outside the home; technology has simplified and lightened the burden of many formerly labor-intensive jobs. The drive toward full equality for women has also been of great benefit, particularly in its emphasis on equal pay and the need to open up jobs hitherto closed to women. But public policies toward blue-collar women have not changed very much; there is still a good deal to be done to ensure that such policies reflect changing realities.

The purpose of the conference was to assess research needs and the role of social science research in helping policy makers understand the special requirements of working-class women. The conference also aimed to encourage cooperation among researchers studying blue-collar, working women and to establish informal communications among them to facilitate access to policy makers in government, education, and unions. To this end, the participants not only exchanged information on their own research, but also offered suggestions for translating their findings into public policy. (It should be noted that the participants' recommendations are not necessarily shared by the Ford Foundation.)

Following is a summary of the main features of the conference.

PANELS

On the first day of the conference four panels, with all participants in attendance, ran successively.

I. Labor Market Problems of Blue-Collar Women. Sally Hillsman Baker, a sociology professor at Queens College in New York City, began the discussion with the comment that working women's problems, hardly touched upon by economists and other analysts, must become more of a public issue. She then reviewed some of the salient facts related to working women:

1) The rate of participation by women in the labor force is increasing, particularly among groups who have not traditionally worked outside the home: older married women and young married women with children. This is especially true in families where the husbands earn below the median national income (estimated by the Department of Commerce to be $12,836 per year for a family of four in 1974).

2) There has been no real change in the disparity between men's and women's ratio of pay. If anything, the gap is widening. One reason is that women workers are often denied the chance to compete for higher-paid jobs. Minority women have even fewer opportunities for good jobs than other women.

3) The traditional separation of men and women in the work force intensified when employers realized that women represented a cheap and reasonably well educated source of available labor.

4) Although evidence indicates that much of the training that prepares workers for advancement occurs on the job, women are rarely given a chance at jobs offering training, usually on the grounds that they have a high rate of turnover and absenteeism. In addition, training is perceived by some employers as reducing the supply of cheap labor. But increased education or training alone will not improve job opportunities for women without a corresponding demand from the labor market for women workers. Inequalities will remain as long as men are in greater demand than women.

Baker concluded that full equality will not occur except under conditions of full employment. Although the present might therefore be considered a bad time to press for equality, she said, it might be a good time to mobilize women around the goal of reducing income discrepancies between them and male workers at each economic level. (She noted, however, that inequalities of family income across class boundaries will doubtless persist.)

Norma Briggs, executive secretary to the Governor's Commission on the Status of Women in Wisconsin, noted that the blue-collar woman is relatively invisible—there is considerable ambiguity even about the meaning of the term. Many wives and daughters of blue-collar workers have white-

---

In the Wisconsin Civil Service and Compensation Plan, probably typical of state governments, a licensed practical nurse is paid precisely the same as a parking-lot attendant and less than a beginning state trooper, who needs only a high school education and some on-the-job training. . . .a beginning stock boy or shipping room clerk (traditionally male jobs) is hired at $141 a month more than a beginning typist. —Norma Briggs

---

collar jobs, although they might be better off financially and work under better conditions in blue-collar jobs. Their reasons for choosing, and staying in, white-collar occupations relates to attitudes toward job status: 1) the college-educated are seen as meriting "higher status" jobs; 2) white-collar workers are able to keep their hands clean; 3) blue-collar work is considered cruder than white-collar work. Daughters of blue-collar workers are taught to aspire to "ladylike" work while "killing time" between school and marriage.

One of the biggest myths concerning women in the labor force, Briggs remarked, is the value of education. Older women tend to believe that the only thing separating them from a higher-paying job is education. Education, however, pays off for men to a far greater extent than it does for women. In dead-end jobs (very often "women's jobs") the only possibility for growth is to leave the job completely and go back to school, at one's own expense, to prepare for a better position. Very few jobs held by women are gained through apprenticeship.

Briggs also pointed out that on-the-job sex segregation affects the rating of jobs. She cited the Dictionary of Occupational Titles, used by government and many private organizations to determine job rankings and salary rates, as proof that many jobs usually held by women are grossly underrated. For instance, in Wisconsin, a beginning typist starts at Rate 1; a beginning stock clerk starts at Rate 4, $141 per month more. A practical nurse earns a salary equivalent to that of a parking-lot attendant, and a beginning police cadet (high school plus one year on-the-job training) has a higher rating than an administrative secretary. Obviously, the laws requiring equal pay for equal work do not cover these sex-linked rating differentials.

There are several possible strategies for dealing with this problem, according to Briggs:

First, research should be undertaken to obtain more information on job stratification.

Second, more women should be encouraged to move into traditionally "male" jobs, including the work of job analysis.

Third, women should find out which jobs are now learned through apprenticeship and which jobs could be added to that list, and then apply for them.

Finally, Briggs said, research should be conducted on the extent to which women's position in the labor force is affected by the fact that much of a woman's traditional work (at home, as a community volunteer, for example) is unpaid.

Eileen Hoffman of The Conference Board pointed out the need to examine the pros and cons of new work schedules and job structures. She mentioned several new scheduling options as examples: the four-day week, flexible working hours (called flex-time), increased part-time work, and shift work. Hoffman noted that many women must work part time, although they lose thereby some fringe benefits such as medical insurance. In addition, part-time work frequently means dead-end employment.

The special problems of minority women were discussed by Alexis Herman, head of Black Women's Employment Program in Atlanta. At every job level, she said, minority women suffer from racism in addition to sexism, and from the effects of high unemployment as well. Research is needed

---

We need to know a lot more about part-time employees—who they are, where they are, how many hours they work. We need to explore the effects of covering part-timers with union benefits and what laws are needed for their protection. Is a part-time work force unstable? Is it necessarily a poor organizing target? —Anne Nelson

---

on the influence of ethnic and racial heritage in determining a minority woman's participation in the labor market, and on the interrelations among education, job satisfaction, and financial rewards among minority women.

Although the women's movement has opened some employment doors, Hoffman said, minority women have remained relatively unaffected. For them, market variables and the availability of child care are crucial issues. Traditional job-finding institutions that purport to service minority groups have not been very effective. In Atlanta, Herman's placement program has placed more black women since 1972 than the Georgia State Employment System has placed in the last forty years.

9

Several other questions require research, Hoffman contended: 1) how to change the self-image and attitude of women that they "must be cuter, shorter, and dumber than men"; 2) how to sustain job-hunting motivation among minority women after repeated job rejections, 3) how to ensure the relevance of existing sources of data (the Women's Bureau has only three publications dealing with minority women).

Jean Fairfax of the NAACP Legal Defense Fund pointed out that there were too few minority group researchers at the conference. She emphasized that the problems of working women in general do not necessarily encompass the special problems of minority working women.

II. Labor Unions. All the members of this panel have conducted research on the factors inhibiting blue-collar women from becoming more active in trade unions. Barbara Wertheimer, who directed a Foundation-supported study of women's underrepresentation in union leadership, pointed out that although women represent 21.7 per cent of union membership, they hold only 5 per cent of the leadership posts. Future studies, she said, should explore ways to overcome barriers to women's union participation.

Past conflicts between the goals and philosophies of the feminist movement and those of trade-union women were reviewed by Connie Kopelov of the Amalgamated Clothing Workers' Education Department. She noted that the gap between the two groups has narrowed recently. For example, labor now supports the Equal Rights Amendment.

Generally, Kopelov said, working-class women worry about child care, occupational health problems, employment security, advancement, and salaries rather than about sexism in general. On issues such as maternity leave and child care, research is needed to determine whether legislation or collective bargaining is the more powerful strategy. Collective bargaining alone does not seem adequate, according to Kopelov, because the job categories that include the majority of women workers are the least organized and the most highly competitive. Further, working women are constantly threatened by nonunion competition.

Disputes over protective legislation for all workers were not ended by Title VII of the 1964 Civil Rights Act, which prohibits employment discrimination on the basis of race, creed, national origin, or sex, Kopelov noted. Research is needed, she said, on how unorganized women workers will be affected by the end of protective legislation covering matters as lifting weights and limited working hours. It is also necessary to determine the problems that must be solved in industrial management if protective legislation is instituted for both men and women workers.

The need for research on the woman activist—her attitudes, characteristics, family responsibilities, age, marital status—was also emphasized by Kopelov. Does the activist represent women workers whose needs and goals may be quite different? Wertheimer added that longitudinal studies

---

Today we see a new self-awareness on the part of working women, particularly labor union women who are trying to move forward in many ways, getting their unions to be more aware of their concerns and moving up into union leadership positions. —Barbara Wertheimer

---

are needed on women taking part in union leadership training programs, and on the problems that all working women must deal with: health, family attitudes and responsibilities, and child care.

Anne Nelson, also of Cornell's School of Industrial and Labor Relations, discussed the relation between the minor participation of women workers in trade unions and their home-related problems. For example, she said, an informal survey by Cornell students revealed that in juggling home duties with a job, working women average only four or five hours of sleep a night. Nelson then cited four other issues that merit continued research: voluntary (as opposed to forced) overtime; paid maternity-pregnancy leave; child-care services, and retraining for women reentering the labor market.

Part-time work is a case in point, Nelson said. If they had the choice, would some full-time women workers prefer part-time employment? If so, what about job security, seniority, and fringe benefits—all central issues for part-time workers. Nelson indicated that unions generally are uninterested in organizing part-time workers, largely because unions associate them with frequent turnover. But, she added, such attitudes toward part-time work should be analyzed. Who are the part-time women workers? Is the part-time labor force really unstable and hard to organize? Which industries are the least flexible in regard to part-time work? Studies are needed, Nelson concluded, on how unions have organized in industries such as retail trade that include many part-time women, and on how benefits can be arranged for part-time workers.

Nelson also posed the question of whether these issues should be resolved through collective bargaining by individual unions, or through national legislation.

The need for women to move into occupations now dominated by men was underlined by Gloria Johnson, education director of the International Union of Electrical Workers (IUE). She recalled that after World War II, the U.S. Labor Board drastically reduced the number of jobs occupied primarily by women. But she recognized the difficulty of reconciling af-

11

firmative action for women workers and union seniority systems, especially during a recession. According to Johnson, full employment is needed for an effective affirmative action program. She alleged that voluntary affirmative action plans, even many of those established by court decisions, have been a sham—designed mainly to give companies a good "image." Men in higher positions usually are the first to hear of new job openings, and they pass that information on to men down the line. One of the goals of the IUE, Johnson said, is to ensure an equitable system of job posting and job bidding. Especially during periods of job scarcity, however, it is necessary to avoid pitting worker against worker, men against women, whites against blacks, and workers against unions.

Johnson said research is needed to determine the effectiveness of "pre-hire seniority"* and compensatory pay to workers who are laid off. Patterns of layoffs in recessions also need to be studied. Among other things we need to know more about is how unemployed women workers survive during layoffs.

III. Blue-Collar Employed Women: Attitudes, Life Conditions, and Dual Roles. American institutions have failed to respond to the culture, values, and needs of working-class people, asserted Nancy Seifer, director of Community Relations at the Institute on Group Identity and Pluralism in New York City. The educational system and the structure of the job market intimidate working-class women and help trap them in a cycle of low self-esteem, she said. Many working-class women lack options, and feel alienated, powerless, and insecure. Many also lack high career aspirations for their children because, with so little outside-the-home satisfaction in their own lives, the family becomes all-important. To them, Seifer said, education means sending children off to another culture and thereby, in effect, losing them.

Laura Lein, a research associate at the Center for the Study of Public Policy in Cambridge, Mass., discussed some of the difficulties that working-class women encounter in their own family life and in arranging for child care. Day care is used infrequently, Lein said, because it is expensive and to some seems to represent an intrusion of alien values into children's lives. And some mothers find it difficult to delegate responsibility for care

*An effort to ease the burden of layoffs, which now fall disproportionately on women and minorities because they lack seniority due to earlier discrimination against them in hiring. With pre-hire seniority, those who applied for jobs after passage of the Civil Rights Act in 1964, but were turned down because of race or sex and then were later hired, could claim as part of their seniority the years between their original application (and discriminatory rejection) and actual hiring.

of children to others because they feel that the children are their own responsibility. Further, Lein noted, wives and husbands who work different hours are limited in their family time together, a factor that may cause the parents to be inconsistent in their child-rearing practices.

Mothers tend to be harsh judges of their own mothering, Lein said. They may not take into account that their irritability toward their children may be related to outside factors, such as frustration on the job or extreme fatigue, caused in part, Lein noted, by the fact that working mothers still tend to shoulder the heavier burden of household responsibility, no matter how household and child-rearing chores are divided.

There is often a degree of self-blame in working at a low-paying, dead-end job, said Mary Lou Finley, a doctoral candidate in the Department of Women's Studies at the University of Puget Sound. Even if working women comprehend their disadvantaged position, they don't do much about it. And in any case, Finley said, blue-collar women tend to see their problems in terms of class, not sex.

The structured inequality in which blue-collar women find themselves can lead to depression and anxiety, according to Lillian Rubin of the

Wright Institute in Berkeley. She pointed out the need to analyze variations within communities of the kinds of advice and assistance available to women. In many parts of the East, for example, ethnic neighborhoods offer a variety of social and religious groups where women can turn to friends for understanding and informal support. Clearly defined ethnic enclaves are rare on the West Coast, however, with the result that working women must find other sources of help.

Rubin said that many working-class women feel "boxed in," unable to confide their problems to others. She concluded that the mechanisms of social and psychological support among working-class women ought to be studied to determine which ones are the most effective and which need to be strengthened.

IV. Health and Safety vs. Equal Opportunity. Leaders of this panel were particularly concerned that legislation currently protecting women from certain health hazards in industry should not be discontinued as a result of Title VII, but should, where applicable, be extended to men as well. Edna Raphael, professor of labor studies at Pennsylvania State University, pointed out that certain controls aimed at protecting women are perhaps partially responsible for women's longer life expectancy. If they were lifted, life expectancies of men and women might become more similar. It is difficult to do research on this, however, she said, since death certificates in the United States (unlike those in many other countries) do not list occupation. Research is also needed, she said, to analyze physiological differences, such as the relative ability to lift weights.

A study done in the early twentieth century on women in industry, which proposed several avenues for research on the occupational health hazards to women workers, was recalled by Cora Marrett, sociology professor at the University of Wisconsin. At that time, certain dramatic events had spurred corrective action on occupational hazards—for example, the discovery that match factory workers handling phosphorus were prone to bone deformity. Today, however, occupational hazards no longer seem so dramatic, with the result that research on the subject seems to have a very low priority in the United States. A more balanced, undramatic approach to research is needed to learn more about health needs associated with women's reproductive function in the contemporary working environment. As a case in point, Vilma Hunt, professor of environmental health at Pennsylvania State University, remarked that the use of radiation in nearly every industry is of particular concern to women of childbearing age because of its possible effect on the health of their unborn children.

Jeanne Stellman of the Oil, Chemical and Atomic Workers International Union, added that there is a shortage of professional expertise on occupational health throughout the country. Although this issue concerns women, it is not a "women's" issue. Hundreds of thousands of workers die from occupational diseases, many of which are not even recognized as such. For example, she said, it was not until 1969 that black lung disease was acknowledged as a hazard associated with mining.

14

Other occupational hazards, such as lead poisoning, are suspected of causing damage to unborn children, Stellman added. Because of such suspicions, the Environmental Health Committee of the Lead Industries Association, a management group, has recommended that women of childbearing age not be employed in the lead industry. Stellman said, however, that such a stance ignores the fact that male workers, too, are susceptible to lead poisoning and to ill effects from even low levels of lead in the work environment. On the other hand, Stellman added, Title VII

I propose that several factors have contributed to the deficiency in the number of studies of health conditions of women workers in this country: (1) The general belief that women workers are usually in a safer environment than are men—a belief not generally true for the blue-collar worker. (2) A common belief that women workers do not appear to show any characteristics of morbidity and mortality that are different from men in the same environment, so that they do not need to be specifically studied. Examination of worker's compensation experience of women is not wholly consistent with this view. (3) A view that women workers change their jobs frequently or leave the work force for extended periods, change their names, or work part time—that they are a "shadow work force" and can be tacitly disregarded. The long-term consistently employed blue-collar woman worker still comes to be included in this generalization. (4) An opinion that the economic value of the woman worker is less—so that expensive study is unwarranted. Current textbooks in occupational health usually have considerably more space allocated to absenteeism than to any of the multitude of physical or social reasons for absenteeism, and certainly far more than is seen on any specific health condition, or on differential effects of toxic substances on women and/or their offspring. (5) Most industrial physicians and research investigators are men and have had very little contact with women in blue-collar jobs. —Vilma R. Hunt

---

must not be used to force women to endanger their health in order to have a job. She stressed that little research has been done on job-related health problems. Hypertension, for example, may be induced by work-related conditions, e.g., noise, fatigue, and psychological stress.

Alice Cook, professor emeritus at Cornell, commented that the United States has lagged behind other countries in adopting legislation to correct acknowledged health problems. She also cited the low status of industrial medicine in America. In addition to the hazards of toxic industrial substances, Cook added, many health problems stem from the fact that most machines are built by men to men's size and build. The effect of this on women workers has not been determined, and should be studied.

WORKSHOPS

On the second day of the conference participants separated into four workshops, which ran concurrently. All were designed to elicit new ideas for research.

I. Community Resources for Blue-Collar Working Women. During this workshop participants stressed that the services women need most are:
  —child care while mothers are working, visiting the doctor, or obtaining other services;
  —coordination of public school hours with their own work schedules;
  —school curricula that reflect the life of working women and working mothers;
  —evening and weekend hours at health and mental health clinics;
  —neighborhood-based health and mental health services;
  —the opportunity to continue their education;
  —informal counseling for family, job, school, and personal problems;
  —low cost, accessible recreation and vacation facilities;
  —more adequate transportation to work and to community and educational facilities;
  —legal aid and lay counselors to mediate between blue-collar women and institutions;
  —information about consumer problems and neighborhood buying clubs;
  —information about how to obtain information.
Discussion centered on the advances other countries have made in providing child care for working mothers. Many, for example, provide care for children of working mothers both before and after school, home-based day care by trained child aides, home-care or day-care center services for moderately sick children, toy and book allowances, and male staff and couples as well as female staff in child-care centers.

Further discussion focused on job training for women reentering the labor market: easing their reentry through reorientation; subsidized retraining; job information and counseling; cash allowances for training, transportation, and clothing, and the need for systematic research on how blue-collar working women view such services and how they can be adapted to local needs and community settings.

16

II. Training and Upgrading. Topics included discrimination against women; support systems for mature women reentering the labor market; the need for changes in vocational education, and resistance to the upward mobility of lower-paid women workers.

It was frequently stated that more research is needed on changes that would make traditional educational systems of greater value to working women. Several panel participants alleged that vocational schools are outmoded and that research is needed on how to change the psychological conditioning of women within the public schools, and on how to alter the training of school counselors.

Norma Briggs noted that women who have had on-the-job training have not necessarily been rewarded by increased salaries on a par with those received by men. The relation between blue-collar women and management should be explored, she said. One purpose would be to learn the response of women to different types of supervision. Another would be to determine whether craft skills are necessary to blue-collar women moving into management.

Other participants noted that training is particularly important during a recession when most people have to "run just to stand still." The question then arose whether affirmative action is helping women receive on-the-job training.

To sum up, participants agreed that research is needed on:
—the quality of life of blue-collar working women;
—services for unemployed women workers;
—meaningful jobs that may become available within the next few decades;
—the relation of societal changes to redefinitions of work;
—variations in work schedules: part-time work, a shorter work week, "flex-time";
—ways to utilize existing job and training information networks;
—training systems for working women in other countries;
—better ways of disseminating job-related research to blue-collar working women.

III. Feminism and the Blue-Collar Employed Woman. This workshop addressed the question: What does feminism mean in a blue-collar setting and how do blue-collar women perceive feminist issues? It was agreed that commonalities among women of all classes may include the need for child care for working mothers, leadership training, improved self-image, availability of continuing education, and more effective legislation for job and family-related activities. It was pointed out, however, that even within the

17

scope of common needs, there may be vast differences in the types of services required by women of differing backgrounds. Some women are hostile to publicly supported institutional child care; they see it as a threat to their image as mothers, and fear the possibility of "alien ideas" being imposed on their children. Or they cannot accept public child care as a permissible way to obtain free time for themselves. Therefore, participants felt, more research is needed on the attitudes of working women regarding the nature, location, and content of child-care services.

Many panelists asserted that occupational improvements necessary for blue-collar women are related more to class than to feminism. Issues important to blue-collar workers regardless of sex are health and safety, organization of nonunion workers, decent pay, autonomy and responsibility at work, and full employment. If the job remains dead-end, it does not matter whether the employer is a man or a woman. It was agreed that the Coalition of Labor Union Women (CLUW), which was formed in 1974 to organize trade union women to demand affirmative action and other job-related programs, is an important potential force for bringing about concrete changes on the job and in job opportunities, subjects on which both feminists and blue-collar women agree.

Panelists also stated that many class-related issues, such as the availability of satisfying work, job security, and pay, affect traditional family structures and attitudes. Since blue-collar women traditionally had few job options, marriage remained the best alternative for many. Consequently, such women have had modest expectations about the quality of marriage relationships. Feminists need to recognize that many women will try to preserve even an oppressive marriage for economic reasons, and that housewives' unpaid work has considerable value. However, certain beliefs prevalent among blue-collar women, such as "marriage is forever" or "I'm only working temporarily," have not held up in the face of contemporary realities, especially the changing nature of family stability. Blue-collar women, no less than many other Americans, are in transition, their values in flux. Research is needed to discover their new attitudes in order to provide services and support systems that will more adequately meet their changing needs.

IV. **Minority Women.** The problems of blue-collar women tend to be lumped together as if the same troubles afflicted all such women identically. But minority women have special employment problems. Discussion focused on the scarcity of information on minority women, the many issues for which there are few or no data, on programs and policies with special implications for minority women, and on the uses of research as a means of learning more about minority women.

It was noted that certain groups of women—American Indians, for instance—are almost completely unstudied. Since many data banks have dumped minority women into an "other" category, there is no breakdown on specific minorities. Statistics are therefore unavailable about the non-involvement in the labor force of some minority women and the kinds of underemployment others experience. There is a need to explore the movement of minority women in and out of the labor force, their shifts from domestic to nondomestic work and from agricultural to industrial employment, and the impact on minority women of changes in the economy.

What are minority women's opinions of their work? Are there special characteristics attached to the kinds of jobs they have, and if so, what are they? Instances of specific job situations are needed to learn where minority women meet resistance and what kinds of support systems exist for them. Research should be done on where and how they seek information about jobs, and how school and vocational counselors prepare them for employment. Where public agencies and employment services have been inadequate in placing minority women in jobs, is it because of lack of interest, lack of monetary resources, or some other cause?

Research is also needed on programs that have been successful in helping minority women and on whether the concepts behind these programs could be applied to other efforts.

More also needs to be known, participants said, about policies that discriminate against minorities entering apprenticeship programs. Many insurance companies make it more costly to hire women because of the high cost of maternity benefits. How does this apply to the particular situation of the minority woman? Black women can be denied employment because they carry a sickle cell anemia trait. Research needs to be done to see if this has been used as an excuse to deny jobs to blacks.

Panelists emphasized the need for action-oriented research to help minority women deal with difficulties encountered in the labor market. Ultimately, of course, the aim is to remove those obstacles; in the meantime, minority women must learn to cope with them. It was agreed that minority women should be involved in the research projects from the outset.

19

CONFERENCE EVALUATION

Participants gathered at the close of the conference to evaluate their discussions and suggest how their research could be better utilized.

Legislative Task Force Proposal. The necessity of the participants' keeping in touch with each other to share information on their projects and findings was unanimously agreed upon. It was concluded that they should organize to influence policy makers and that a task force or clearinghouse should be established to work with congressional committees and other legislative organizations.* Its purpose would be to supply data for testimony and to help conduct hearings and public meetings on issues of concern to working women. Researchers and activists, as well as policy makers, need information about legal, legislative, and contractual developments and decisions that affect women workers. A task force or clearinghouse could also disseminate information on national and local policies and projects. A central office, perhaps in cooperation with the Coalition of Labor Union Women, could be set up in Washington, D.C., to concentrate on problems of wage-earning women, as the National Manpower Policy Task Force does for men.

Conference and Research Activities. Participants were concerned that blue-collar working women, and especially wage-earning minority women, be better represented at future conferences. More minority women scholars should be encouraged to conduct research, and a fellowship program for them was suggested as one means of bringing this about. Lectures should be sponsored in various parts of the country on the particular problems of minority women workers.

Other suggestions included:

—developing shorter, more popularized research output;

—researching problems of white-collar women;

—developing contacts with women in other fields;

—holding an annual national meeting on problems of blue-collar women;

—developing regional research meetings;

—inviting congressional and other legislative staff persons to attend the national or regional meetings.

*Such a task force is in the process of being established. Ed.

20

CLOSING REMARKS

Alice Cook, Professor Emeritus, Cornell University

We have set ourselves a formidable task and selected large issues to talk about—issues that involve sex and class struggle. As a group, we do not normally undertake this kind of activity, although we are both scholars and activists. We have tried, in the first place, to go beyond and behind the facts, articulate them, share them, document them, and footnote them. Then we have tried to distill the priority issues in order to state specifically the kind of action to be taken to realize policy change.

The Diversity Among Us. We tend to talk about blue-collar women as though they were a single "category," but very early on one of our sisters reminded us that there is great variety within this group, and that we were in danger of superimposing upon it a monolithic concept that assumes blue-collar women to be whites, a subgroup whose characteristics and needs must be differentiated from minorities.

In dealing with the special problems of women, the tendency is to speak of them as though they were frozen at one stage of their lives. We forget that we are dealing with a phenomenon called roving statistics. A few years ago, Alva Myrdal and Viola Klein said that women play different roles in various phases of adult life. I think that although those phases have changed in their dimensions, it remains true that some women work before marriage, when their children are small, and while their children are growing up. Then there are other women who go to work because the child-rearing function has been completed—women who are taken into the work force not to support children, but because they have no more children to support. Work is meant to fill that gap.

The influx of women, especially married women and mothers, into the labor force constitutes a major structural change that is proceeding so fast that the statistics are lagging way behind the fact. Thus we have to be trend spotters as well as trend analyzers. Many times we learn a great many facts from this trend-spotting process that will only be documentable years later, long after our articles have appeared.

The Female Work Force. Our main problem now is that we are working in an area that has often been described in male nouns and pronouns—

21

manpower, for example. The result is that the female labor force, with its special characteristics, has not been independently identified and characterized. We need to look at the special life cycle of women at work: entry, exit, reentry, and the fact that the length of women's absence from the labor market varies from country to country and within our own country. Indeed, the time away from the labor market seems to be compressing in this country to a very few years.

The very fact of leaving and then returning to the labor market is one of the major characteristics that differentiates women workers from men workers. Women interrupt and men do not interrupt their work lives, and so we have a special labor market problem, i.e., all the norms of the labor market have been set to conform to the kind of work lives that men lead, uninterrupted from school to retirement. Women cannot conform to that.

We have not really looked at the labor market as an institution comprising persons of different qualifications, differing life cycles, differing periods of work. Many of us have not learned to look at the interrupted career as an acceptable career. We keep trying to make up for the shortcomings that women must invariably face because they are not men.

Men and women all over the Western world take great pride in saying that in our labor market women can choose to work or not to work. This is a very nice idea, and one that prevails in all of the non-Communist countries. But women have paid a high price for a choice they can exercise only in a narrow range. If they choose to go to work and cannot at the same time fulfill all their regular household functions, that is considered to be their problem; society does not feel it owes them any particular kind of support. They and they alone will have to pay for child care and for their training or retraining. They must pay for being different from men.

One of the reports that affected me most during this conference was on the job classification system from the Dictionary of Occupational Titles, which reflects the male norm. This particularly affected me because I have been looking historically at the question of equal pay, and I realize that the International Labor Organization, in its efforts to have all the nations of the world conform to the standard of equal pay, places great emphasis on job classification as the scientific tool that can be used to make women's earnings equal to men's. We have seen that even this tool has to be re-examined.

I suspect that there is no element in the labor-market vocabulary, the labor-market institution, or in labor-market history and structure that will not have to be restated in order to accommodate women. That is one of our major tasks, and one on which we are well launched.

22

Societal Sex Reeducation. The second issue that is being considered very seriously in many other countries is the whole problem of sex role reeducation. When the Swedes began to take their "new look" at the labor market and at women's place and role in society, they started with the educational system. School texts were rewritten to teach sexual equality. By starting at the very early levels of education, they hoped that boys and girls would not be so sex-imprinted, jobs wouldn't be sex-imprinted, and job aspirations wouldn't be sex-imprinted, as they customarily had been. Over the short haul and the middle haul, but let us hope not over the long haul, we are going to have to deal with the problem in this way, because people do not quickly or accidentally change such fundamental and deeply imbedded attitudes.

As for specific, immediate issues, the field of national health services deserves priority attention, I think, partly because of the times we live in, partly because of the readiness of Congress to deal with it, but also because of its basic significance for women. It is clear that women who work and run households are carrying a double burden and are under stresses that are probably far greater than those of men in the labor market. This means a growing set of problems in mental and physical health for women, problems that must be met in our plans for a national health service.

Another consideration for our agenda is that we are the only modern industrial nation that does not provide for paid maternity leave. We are behind the times and behind other countries in the world. I think paid maternity leave is the next very big issue. Once we have that, enormous stress will be lifted from women, most of whom want to be mothers, but can only be mothers at the price of careful financial planning and often financial deprivation.

Paid child-care leave is another important issue that I think we need to consider as an alternative, or even as a supplement, to child care in all its manifestations: preschool care, after-school care, vacation care, care of sick children, etc.

The vast significance to women workers of such dangers as industrial toxic exposures has been impressed on us in the discussions of this conference. I think the next thing on the agenda must be the monitoring not only of programs such as those under Title VII, but also of the Occupational Safety and Health Act.

We are moving into a period of great economic change, which is not necessarily all progress and hope; the shadow of the 1930s Depression lies over us. It affects us not only economically; it also challenges the few important gains women made in the 1960s and 1970s, which were incorporated into a group of laws dealing with equal pay and equal opportunity. It has been demonstrated to us here that we may indeed be facing very serious choices in respect to retaining these gains.

My recent study of equal pay in several countries* has led me to the conclusion that the U.S. may be ahead of all other countries with respect to equal pay and equal opportunity. We have a battery of laws and, finally, since 1972, a set of enforcement procedures that, if used aggressively, may really be able to get women ahead. I think we have the tools, if we know how to use them, but these tools are in danger in an economic recession. The whole issue of seniority versus equal opportunity under Title VII is a case in point.

We have to look at what kind of guidance counseling our schools offer to women. Next on the agenda, therefore, I would list an attempt to move into the school-guidance systems of this country, with retraining of guidance and vocational counselors, to recognize that women have very special needs. And not just school counseling, but also the vocational counseling available to working women as they reenter the labor force, need reconsideration. Careers, including possibilities for growth, skill development, and promotion, must be possible for women who begin work at 30 or 35 and have 30 or 35 years of work life ahead of them. They and their employers who look at their futures in these terms can well afford a substantial investment of money and time in their careers.

What Kind of Women's Movement? Next among our objectives should be the question of the kind of women's movement we ought to build in this country. Shall it be a movement of working women, of working-class women, of women generally?

Although these are not necessarily opposites or exclusives, most issues involve the question of whether we are going to put our main emphasis on national alliances or on local action within our own neighborhoods and through our personal contacts.

One strategic question is whether working women should cooperate in alliances of blue-collar women generally, of labor unions only, or with all kinds of women's organizations. When the Australian women set up their organization two years ago, they expressly decided to avoid, if they could, the American splintering of women's groups. As a result they include blue-collar, trade-union women as well as professionals. The labor movement in

---

*An abbreviated version of the study, "Equal Pay, Where Is It?" appeared in the May, 1975 issue of the *Industrial Relations Journal* (University of California). Ed.

this country a few years ago rejected the Equal Rights Amendment and favored protective legislation for women; the middle-class women's movement favored ERA and wanted to do away with protective legislation. Some of those opposite views are melting and thinning, and the question of alliances thus becomes less difficult. We need, I believe, to make alliances as broadly as possible, alliances that will represent as much power and influence as we can possibly muster.

Strategy. One of the most important questions will be that of strategy. What are the most important cases to test? I have just heard, for instance, that a group is forming in San Francisco to test the availability of apprenticeships to women. It may be a landmark case. It will, inevitably, be an important measure of the availability of jobs for women in the highly skilled trades.

To put it boldly, I think we have to translate everything we do into political action. We are dealing in the last analysis with political issues. To deny or circumvent that is to delude ourselves.

I hope very much that it will be possible for us to continue our joint work and to implement our common interest by establishing a clearing-house extending beyond the group gathered at this conference. The interest and information we have shared here have helped us all. We can only profit by remaining in contact with each other and widening our circle. It was with great pride and joy that I participated in this conference. I have the sense that we all share this feeling.

PARTICIPANTS

Sally Hillsman Baker
Assistant Professor
Department of Sociology
Queens College
Flushing, New York 11367

Susan Berresford
Program Officer
The Ford Foundation
320 East 43rd Street
New York, New York 10017

Norma Briggs
Executive Secretary
Governor's Commission on
    the Status of Women
1 West Wilson Street
Madison, Wisconsin 53702

Sol Chafkin
Officer in Charge
Social Development
The Ford Foundation
320 East 43rd Street
New York, New York 10017

Herschelle Challenor
Program Officer
The Ford Foundation
320 East 43rd Street
New York, New York 10017

Alice Cook
Professor Emeritus
Cornell University
75 Turkey Hill Road
Ithaca, New York 14850

Ana Del Toro
Field Representative
Recruitment and Training Program
162 Fifth Avenue
New York, New York 10010

Jean Fairfax
Director, Division of Legal
    Information and Community
NAACP Legal Defense and
    Education Fund, Inc.
10 Columbus Circle
New York, New York 10019

Jennie Farley
Assistant Professor
Industrial and Labor Relations
Director, Women's Studies Program
Cornell University
Ithaca, New York 14850

Myra Marx Ferree
Ph.D. Candidate
Department of Psychology and
    Social Relations
Harvard University
33 Kirkland Street
Cambridge, Massachusetts 02138

Mary Lou Finley
Ph.D. Candidate
Department of Women's Studies
University of Puget Sound
Tacoma, Washington 98416

Lois Gray
Assistant Dean
New York State School of Industrial
    and Labor Relations
Cornell University
New York, New York 10017

Alexis Herman
Director
Black Women's Employment
    Program
52 Fairlie Street, N.E.
Atlanta, Georgia 30303

Eileen Hoffman
Associate Specialist in Labor
    Relations Research
The Conference Board
845 Third Avenue
New York, New York 10022

Louise Kapp Howe
Writer
345 East 57th Street
New York, New York 10021

Vilma R. Hunt
Associate Professor of
    Environmental Health
The Pennsylvania State University
114 Human Development Building
University Park, Pennsylvania 16802

Robin Jacoby
Assistant Professor of History
University of Michigan
Ann Arbor, Michigan 48104

Gloria Johnson
Education Director
International Union of
    Electrical Workers
1126 Sixteenth Street, N.W.
Washington, D.C. 20036

Connie Kopelov
Associate National Education
    Director
Amalgamated Clothing Workers
    of America
15 Union Square
New York, New York 10003

Joyce L. Kornbluh
Director, Program on Women
    and Work
Institute of Labor and Industrial
    Relations
University of Michigan
401 Fourth Street
Ann Arbor, Michigan 48103

Judith Long Laws
Assistant Professor of Psychology
    and Sociology
New York State School of
    Industrial and Labor Relations
Cornell University
Ithaca, New York 14850

Laura Lein
Research Associate
Center for the Study of Public Policy
123 Mt. Auburn Street
Cambridge, Massachusetts 02138

Cora Bagley Marrett
Associate Professor
University of Wisconsin-Madison
Department of Sociology
Social Science Building
Madison, Wisconsin 53706

Kathryn H. Mitchell
Assistant Administrative Officer
The Ford Foundation
320 East 43rd Street
New York, New York 10017

Anne Nelson
Associate Director
Trade Union Women's Studies
New York State School of
    Industrial and Labor Relations
Cornell University
New York, New York 10017

Brigid O'Farrell
Coordinator, Women in Crafts
The New England Telephone
    Learning Center
280 Lock Drive
Marlboro, Massachusetts 01752

Edna Raphael
Associate Professor of Labor
    Studies and Sociology
Pennsylvania State University
206 Liberal Arts Building
University Park, Pennsylvania 16802

Pamela Roby
Chairperson, Board of Studies in
    Community Studies
University of California
Santa Cruz, California 95064

Lillian B. Rubin
The Wright Institute
Berkeley, California 94704

Robert Schrank
Project Specialist
The Ford Foundation
320 East 43rd Street
New York, New York 10017

Mary Stevenson
Professor
University of Massachusetts
    at Boston
Boston, Massachusetts 02125

Nancy Seifer
Director, Community Relations
Institute on Group Identity
    and Pluralism
165 East 56th Street
New York, New York 10022

Patricia Sexton
Professor of Sociology
New York University Graduate
    School of Arts and Science
New York, New York 10003

Freya Sonenstein
Ph.D. Candidate, Boston University
Instructor of Sociology
St. Joseph College
1678 Asylum Avenue
West Hartford, Connecticut 06117

Ruth Harris Soumah
Assistant Director
Labor Affairs Program
National Urban League
477 Madison Avenue
New York, New York 10022

Jeanne Stellman
Presidential Assistant for
    Health and Safety
Oil, Chemical and Atomic Workers
International Union
Box 2812
Denver, Colorado 80201

Mitchell Sviridoff
Vice President, Division of
    National Affairs
The Ford Foundation
320 East 43rd Street
New York, New York 10017

Lucretia Dewey Tanner
Senior Labor Economist
Office of Technical Services
Federal Mediation and Conciliation
    Services — U.S. Government
Washington, D.C. 20427

Sheila Tobias
Associate Provost
Wesleyan University
Middletown, Connecticut 06457

Kathryn E. Walker
Professor
New York State College of
    Human Ecology
Cornell University
Ithaca, New York 14850

Basil J. Whiting
Program Officer
The Ford Foundation
320 East 43rd Street
New York, New York 10017

Rachelle Warren
Assistant Research Scientist
Institute of Industrial and
    Labor Relations
University of Michigan
Ann Arbor, Michigan 48103

Barbara Wertheimer
Director
Trade Union Women's Studies
New York State School of
    Industrial and Labor Relations
Cornell University
New York, New York 10017

1461-8
5-27